The Sounds Of Christmas

EASY PIANO

By DAN COATES

Project Manager: Carol Cuellar
Art Direction: Frank Milone
Cover Design: Debbie Lipton
Cover Photo: ©1995 White/Packert, The Image Bank So.

Contents

HAVE YOURSELF
A MERRY LITTLE CHRISTMAS

Words and Music by
HUGH MARTIN and
RALPH BLANE
Arranged by DAN COATES

4

ALL I WANT FOR CHRISTMAS IS
MY TWO FRONT TEETH

Words and Music by
DON GARDNER
Arranged by DAN COATES

ANGELS, FROM THE REALM OF GLORY

Words by
JAMES MONTGOMERY

Music by
HENRY SMART
Arranged by DAN COATES

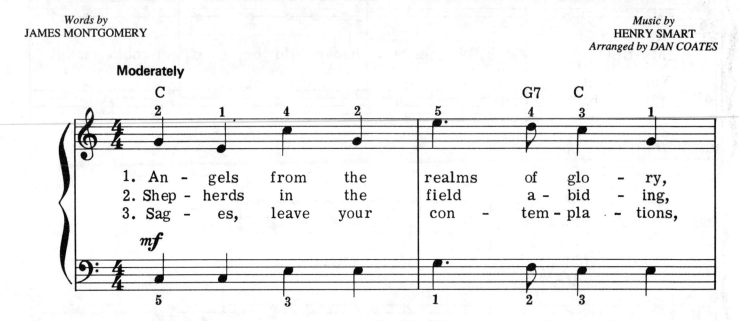

1. An - gels from the realms of glo - ry,
2. Shep - herds in the field a - bid - ing,
3. Sag - es, leave your con - tem - pla - tions,

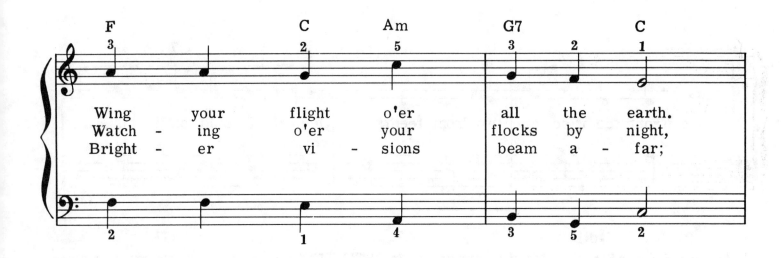

Wing your flight o'er all the earth.
Watch - ing o'er your flocks by night,
Bright - er vi - sions beam a - far;

Ye, who sang cre - a - tion's sto - ry,
God with man is now re - sid - ing,
Seek the great De - sire of na - tions,

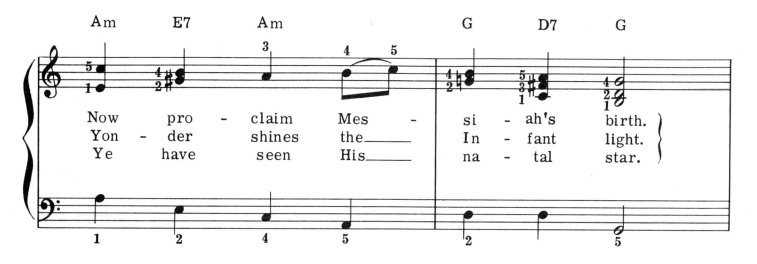

Now pro - claim Mes - si - ah's birth.
Yon - der shines the___ In - fant light.
Ye have seen His___ na - tal star.

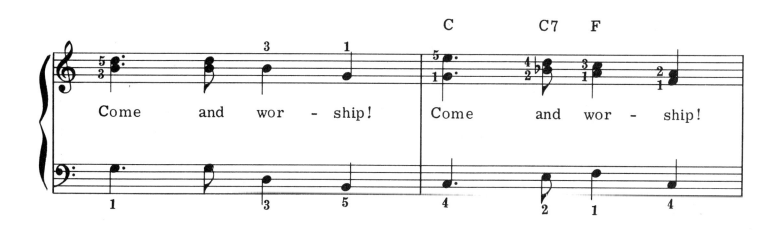

Come and wor - ship! Come and wor - ship!

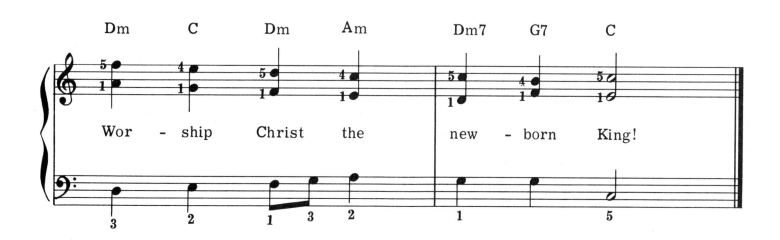

Wor - ship Christ the new - born King!

THE ANNUAL ANIMAL CHRISTMAS BALL

Words and Music by
GEORGE DAVID WEISS
Arranged by DAN COATES

12

13

AWAY IN A MANGER

By
MARTIN LUTHER
Arranged by DAN COATES

GRANDMA GOT RUN OVER
BY A REINDEER!

Words and Music by
RANDY BROOKS
Arranged by DAN COATES

Moderately bright

Grand - ma got run o - ver by a rein - deer walk - ing home from our house Christ - mas

Eve. You can say there's no such thing as San - ta, but

as for me and Grand - pa we be - lieve. 1. She'd been drink - ing too much

egg - nog ____ and we begged her not to go,

Verse 2:
Now we're all so proud of Grandpa,
He's been taking this so well.
See him in there watching football,
Drinking beer and playing cards with Cousin Mel.
It's not Christmas without Grandma.
All the family's dressed in black,
And we just can't help but wonder:
Should we open up her gifts or send them back?

(To Chorus:)

Verse 3:
Now the goose is on the table,
And the pudding made of fig,
And the blue and silver candles,
That would just have matched the hair in Grandma's wig.
I've warned all my friends and neighbors,
Better watch out for yourselves.
They should never give a licence
To a man who drives a sleigh and plays with elves.

(To Chorus:)

THE BIRTHDAY OF A KING

By
WILLIAM H. NEIDLINGER
Arranged by DAN COATES

lu - ia, _____ Oh, how the an - gels sang! Al - le -

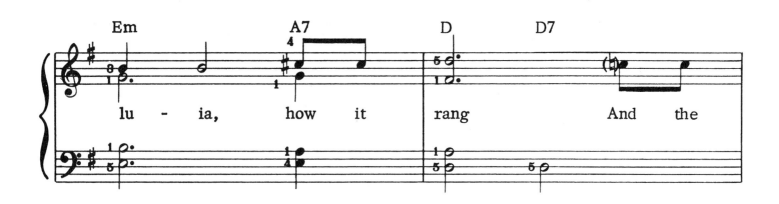

lu - ia, how it rang And the

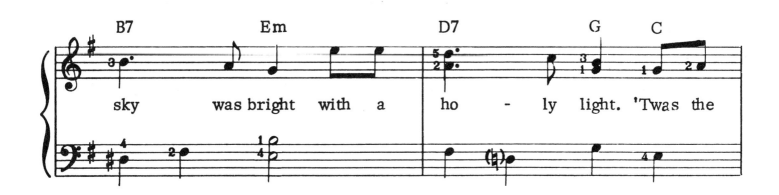

sky was bright with a ho - ly light. 'Twas the

birth - day of a King! 'Twas a King!

A CHILD THIS DAY IS BORN

Traditonal
English
Arranged by DAN COATES

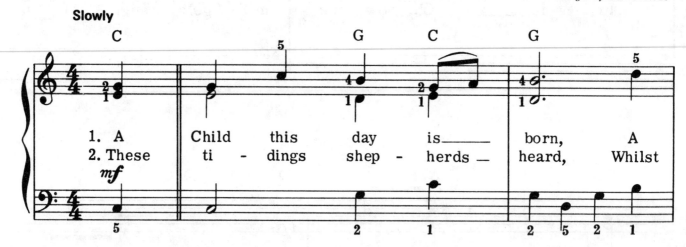

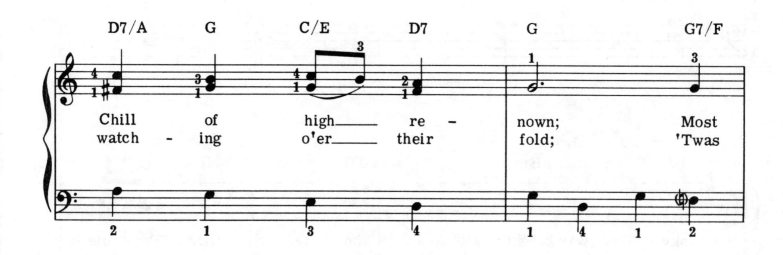

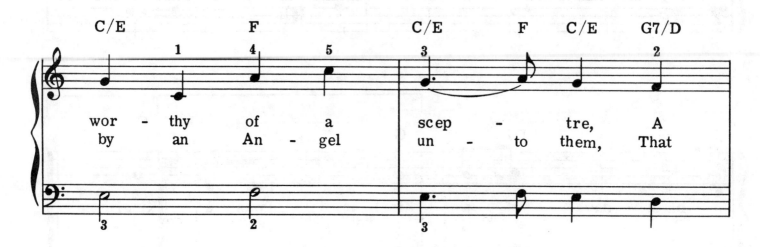

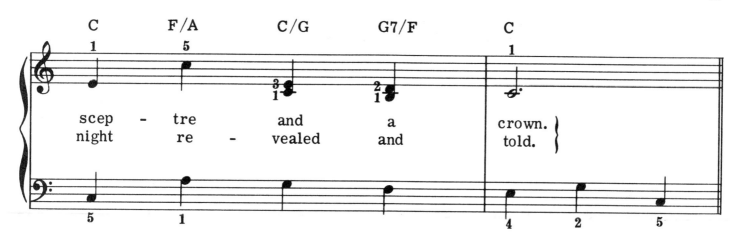

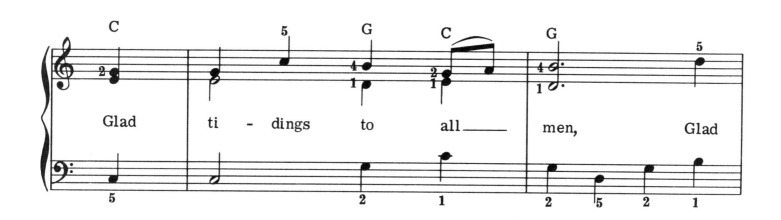

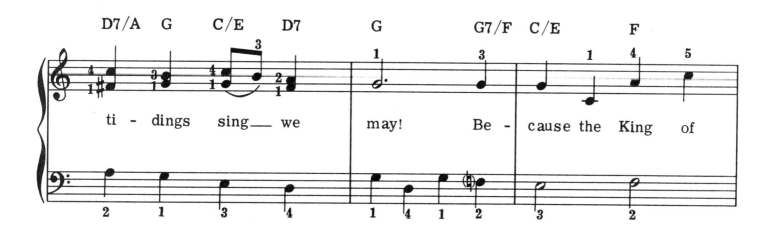

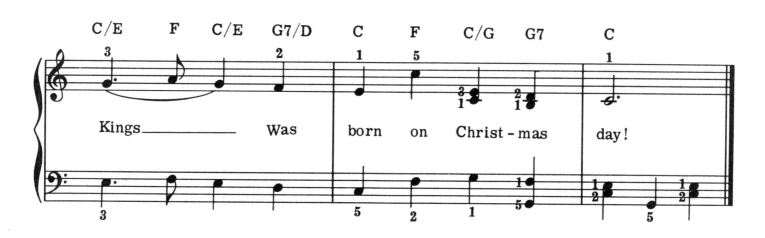

THE CHIPMUNK SONG
(Christmas, Don't Be Late)

By
ROSS BAGDASARIAN, SR.
Arranged by DAN COATES

Moderate waltz ♩. = 52

Christ - mas, Christ - mas time is near,
(2nd time, see additional lyrics)

time for joy and time for cheer.

We've been good, but we can't last.

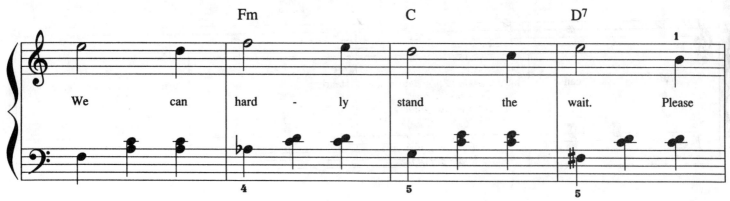

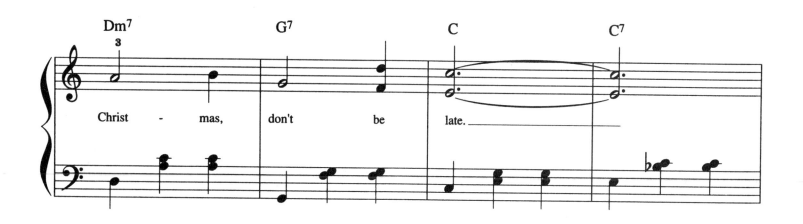

Christ - mas, don't be late. _____

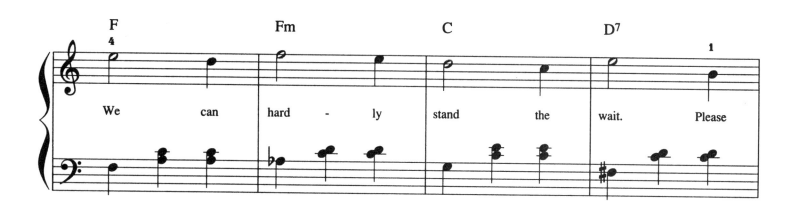

We can hard - ly stand the wait. Please

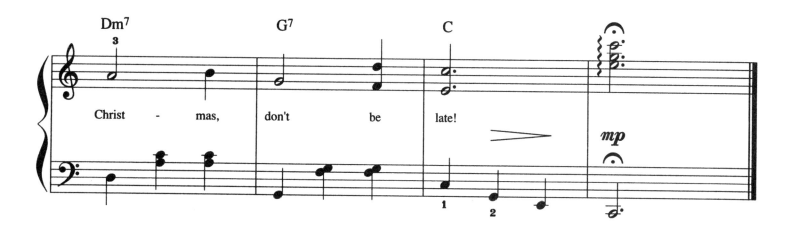

Christ - mas, don't be late!

Additional lyrics (spoken):
Alvin: *Dave, I've been asking for that hula hoop for years.*
I would like to ask for something new,
Like roller skates, or a new stereo.
But I've just got to get that hula hoop first.
Please, Dave?
I feel I've been very patient.
Dave: *Alvin, just finish the song.*
We'll talk about it later.

CHRISTMAS AULD LANG SYNE

Words and Music by
MANN CURTIS and FRANK MILITARY
Arranged by DAN COATES

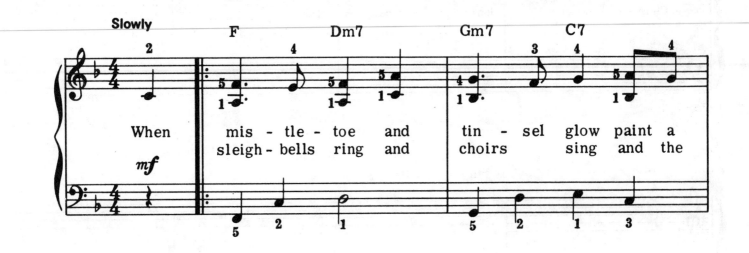

When mis - tle - toe and tin - sel glow paint a
sleigh - bells ring and choirs sing and the

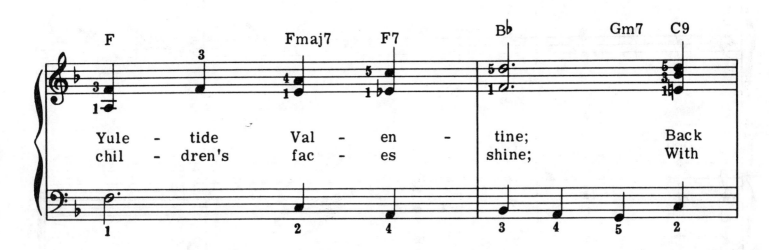

Yule - tide Val - en - tine; Back
chil - dren's fac - es shine; With

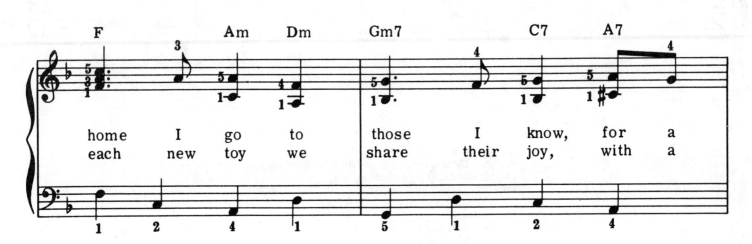

home I go to those I know, for a
each new toy we share their joy, with a

CHRISTMAS IN KILLARNEY

Words and Music by
JOHN REDMOND, JAMES CAVANAUGH
and FRANK WELDON
Arranged by DAN COATES

Moderately

The hol - ly green, the i - vy green, The

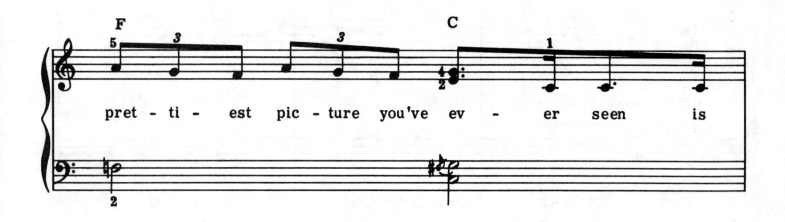

pret - ti - est pic - ture you've ev - er seen is

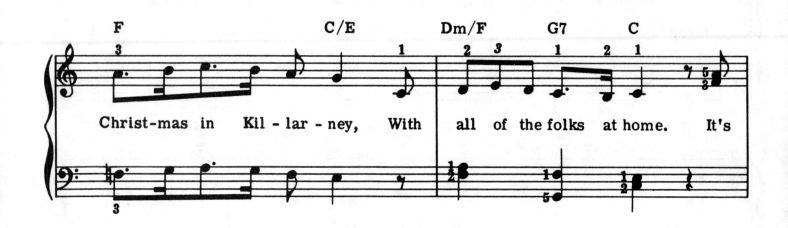

Christ-mas in Kil - lar - ney, With all of the folks at home. It's

nice you know, to kiss your beau while cud-dling un-der the mis-tle-toe, And

San-ta Claus, you know of course, is one of the boys from home. The

door is al-ways o-pen, The neigh-bors pay a call, and

Fa-ther John, be-fore he's gone, Will bless the house and all. How

CHRISTMAS MEM'RIES

Words by
ALAN and MARILYN BERGMAN

Music by
DON COSTA
Arranged by DAN COATES

CHRISTMAS TIME OF YEAR

Words by
JOE COCUZZO

Music by
JOE COCUZZO and TORRIE ZITO
Arranged by DAN COATES

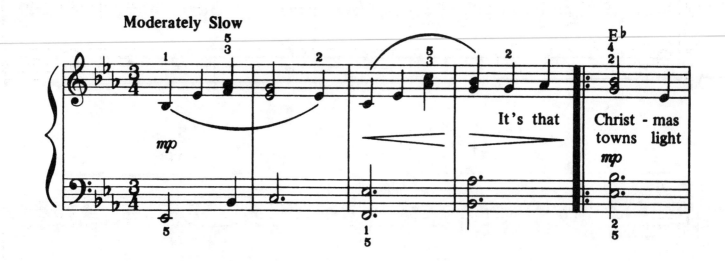

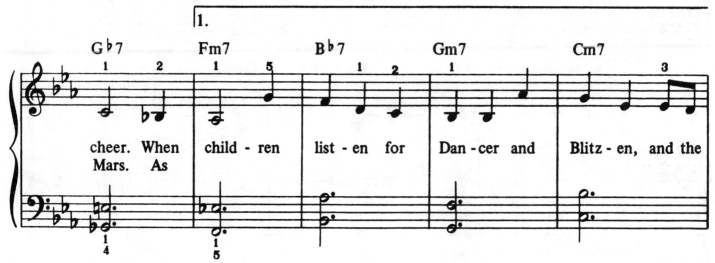

D. S. 𝄋 al Coda ⊕

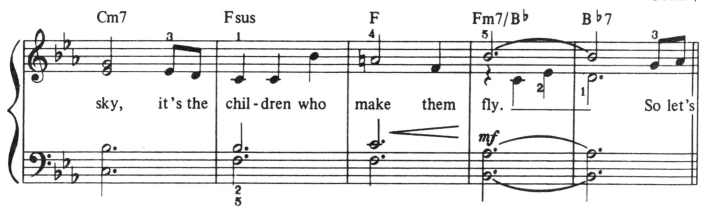

sky, it's the chil-dren who make them fly. So let's

Coda

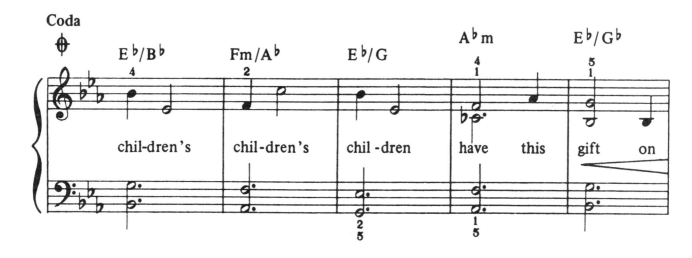

chil-dren's chil-dren's chil-dren have this gift on

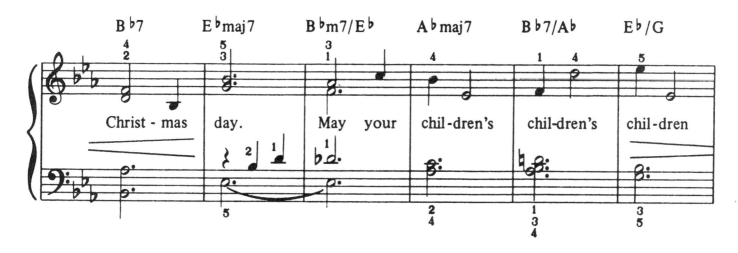

Christ-mas day. May your chil-dren's chil-dren's chil-dren

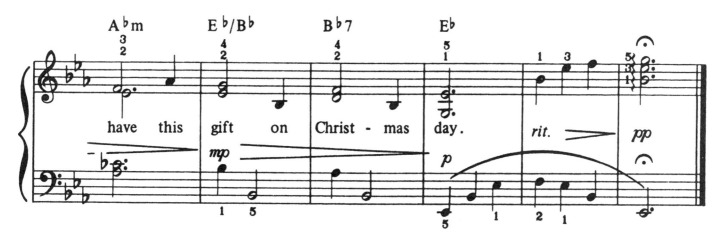

have this gift on Christ-mas day.

THE CHRISTMAS WALTZ

Words by
SAMMY CAHN

Music by
JULE STYNE
Arranged by DAN COATES

41

DECK THE HALL

Traditional Old Welsh
Arranged by DAN COATES

Joyfully

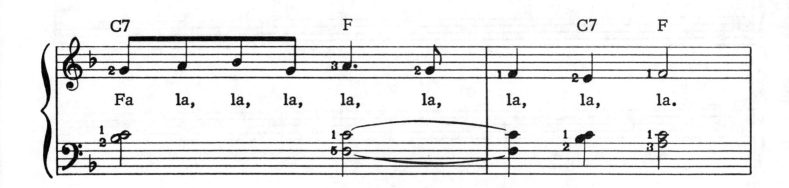

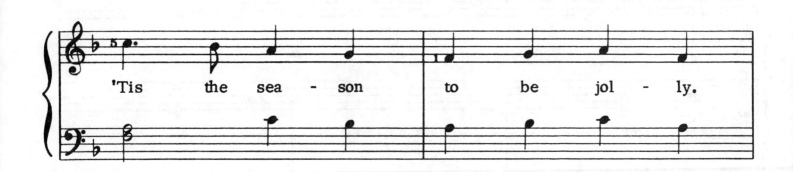

43

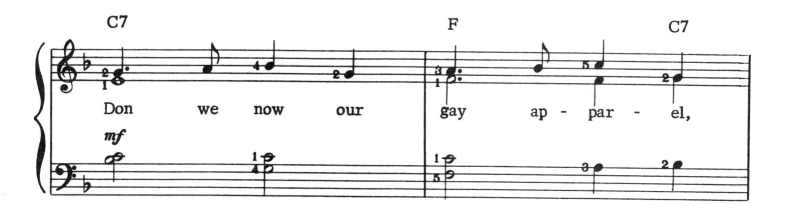

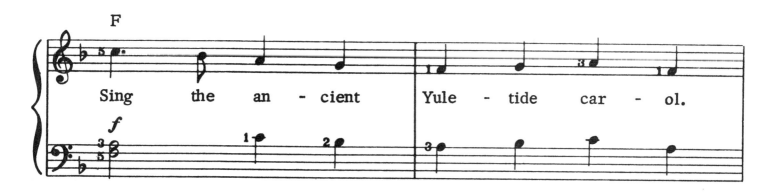

FROM EVERY SPIRE ON CHRISTMAS EVE

Words by
ELEANOR A. HUNTER

Music by
GEORGE COLES
Arranged by DAN COATES

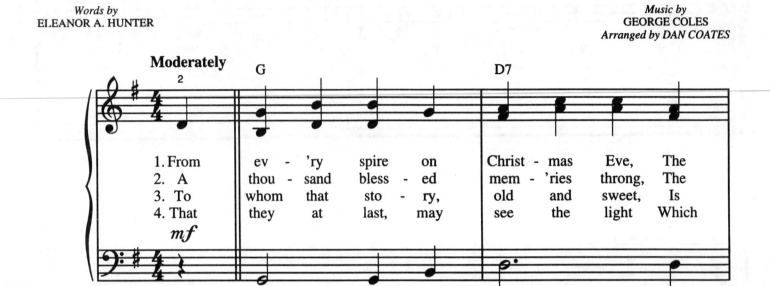

1. From ev - 'ry spire on Christ - mas Eve, The
2. A thou - sand bless - ed mem - 'ries throng, The
3. To whom that sto - ry, old and sweet, Is
4. That they at last, may see the light Which

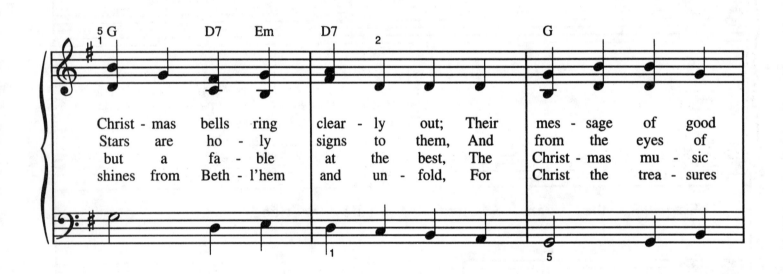

Christ - mas bells ring clear - ly out; Their mes - sage of good
Stars are ho - ly signs to them, And from the eyes of
but a fa - ble at the best, The Christ - mas mu - sic
shines from Beth - l'hem and un - fold, For Christ the trea - sures

will and peace, With man - y a call__ and__ sil - ver shout. For
ev - 'ry child Looks forth the Babe__ of__ Beth - le - hem. But
mocks their ears, And life has naught__ of__ joy or rest. Oh!
of their hearts, Rich - er than spi - cer - y or gold. Hope

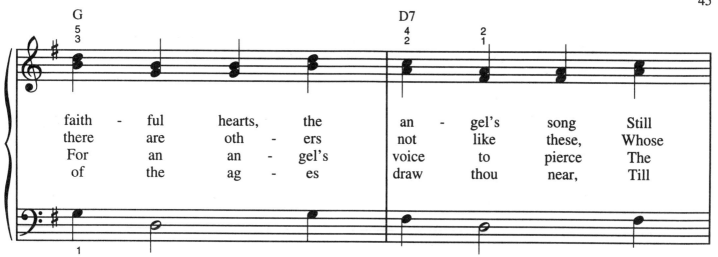

faith - ful hearts, the | an - gel's song Still
there are oth - ers | not like these, Whose
For an an - gel's | voice to pierce The
of the ag - es | draw thou near, Till

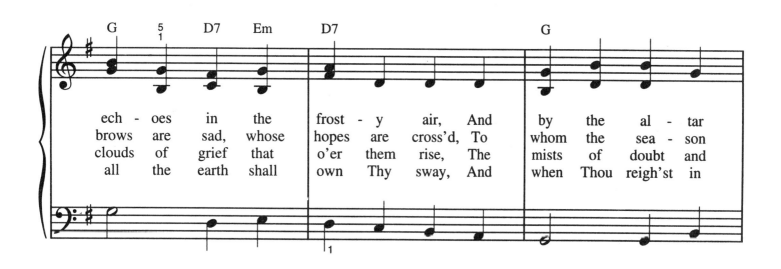

ech - oes in the | frost - y air, And | by the al - tar
brows are sad, whose | hopes are cross'd, To | whom the sea - son
clouds of grief that | o'er them rise, The | mists of doubt and
all the earth shall | own Thy sway, And | when Thou reigh'st in

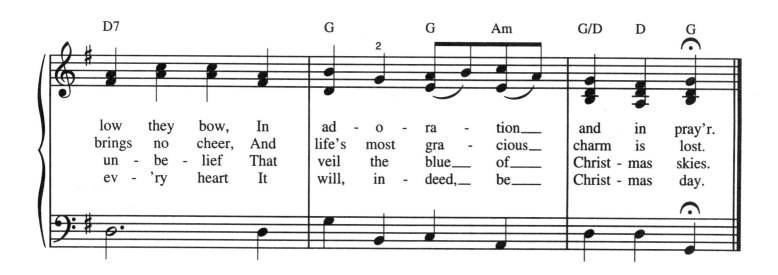

low they bow, In | ad - o - ra - tion___ | and in pray'r.
brings no cheer, And | life's most gra - cious___ | charm is lost.
un - be - lief That | veil the blue___ of___ | Christ - mas skies.
ev - 'ry heart It | will, in - deed,___ be___ | Christ - mas day.

GATHER AROUND THE CHRISTMAS TREE

By
JOHN HOPKINS
Arranged by DAN COATES

Gath - er a - round the Christ - mas tree! Gath - er a - round the

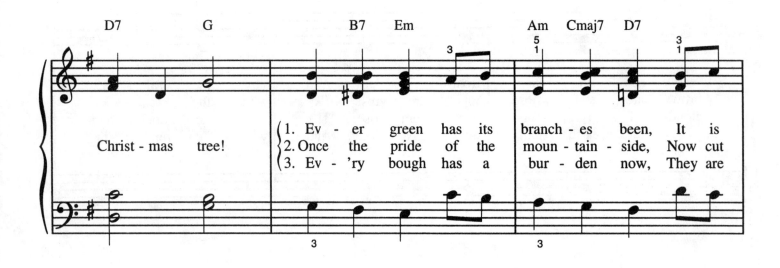

Christ - mas tree!
1. Ev - er green has its branch - es been, It is
2. Once the pride of the moun - tain - side, Now cut
3. Ev - 'ry bough has a bur - den now, They are

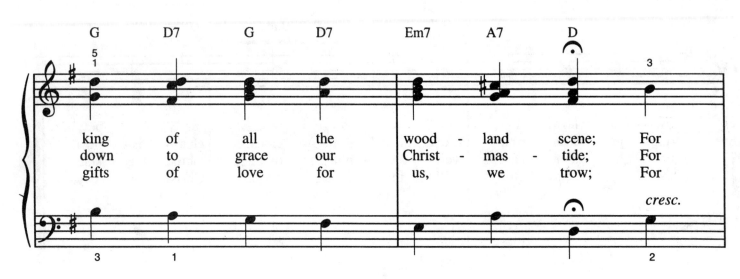

king of all the wood - land scene; For
down to grace our Christ - mas - tide; For
gifts of love for us, we trow; For

GESU BAMBINO
(The Infant Jesus)

Words by
FREDERICK H. MARTENS

Music by
PIETRO A. YON
Arranged by DAN COATES

GLAD CHRISTMAS BELLS

Traditional
Arranged by DAN COATES

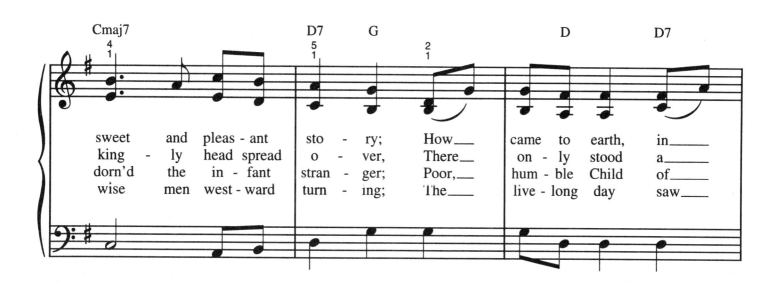

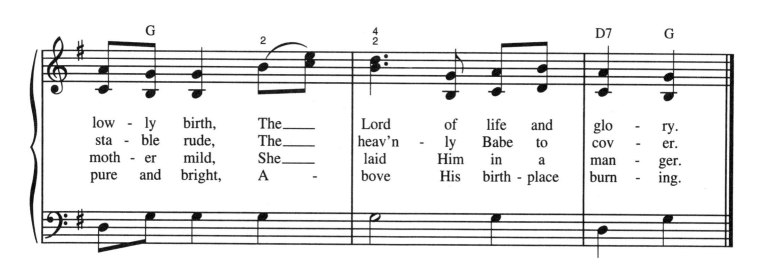

A GREAT AND MIGHTY WONDER

GERMAN
Arranged by DAN COATES

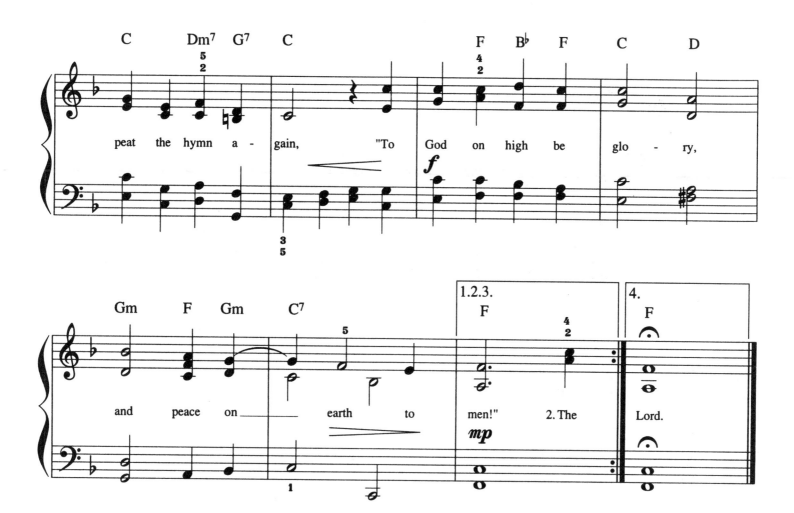

Verse 2:
The Word becomes incarnate
And yet remains on high!
And cherubim sing anthems
To shepherds from the sky. *(Chorus:)*

Verse 3:
While thus they sing your Monarch,
Those bright angelic bands
Rejoice, ye vales and mountains,
Ye oceans, clap your hands. *(Chorus:)*

Verse 4:
Since all He comes to ransom,
By all be He adorned.
The infant born in Bethlehem,
The Savior and the Lord.   *(Chorus:)*

HAIL TO THE LORD'S ANOINTED

Words by
JAMES MONTGOMERY

Music by
L. VAN BEETHOVEN
from "Ninth Symphony"
Arranged by DAN COATES

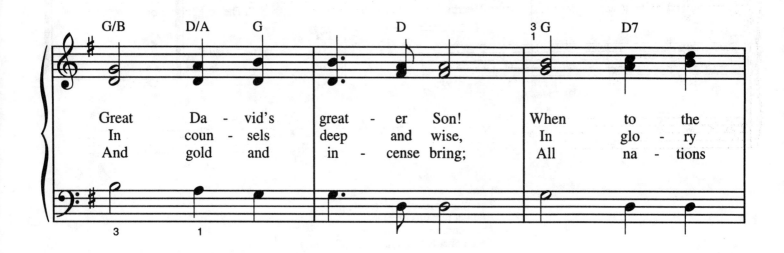

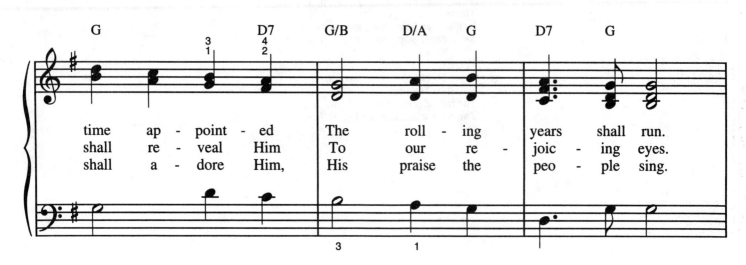

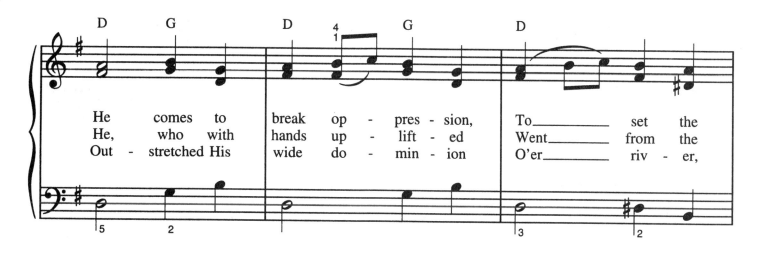

HERE COMES SANTA CLAUS
(Right Down Santa Claus Lane)

Words and Music by
GENE AUTRY and
OAKLEY HALDEMAN
Arranged by DAN COATES

Moderately bright

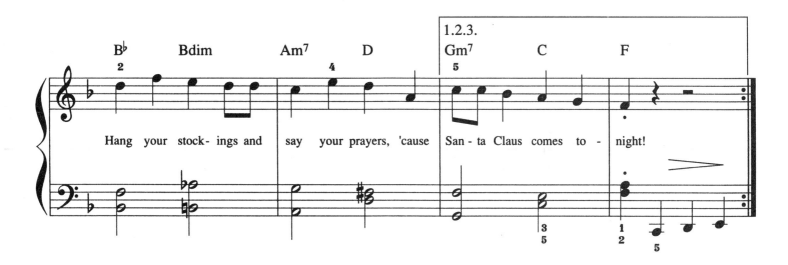

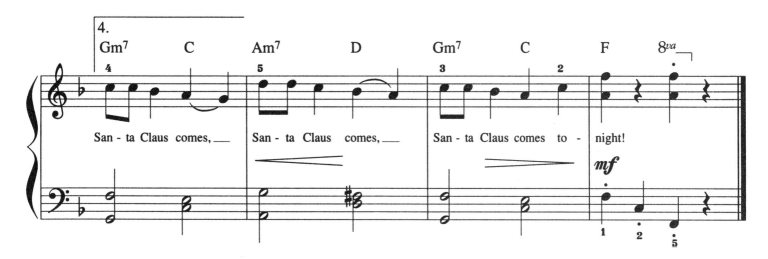

Verse 2:
Here comes Santa Claus! Here comes Santa Claus! Right down Santa Claus Lane!
He's got a bag that is filled with toys for the boys and girls again.
Hear those sleigh bells jingle jangle, what a beautiful sight.
Jump in bed, cover up your head, 'cause Santa Claus comes tonight!

Verse 3:
Here comes Santa Claus! Here comes Santa Claus! Right down Santa Claus Lane!
He doesn't care if you're rich or poor for he loves you just the same.
Santa knows that we're God's children, that makes everything right.
Fill your hearts with a Christmas cheer, 'cause Santa Claus comes tonight!

Verse 4:
Here comes Santa Claus! Here comes Santa Claus! Right down Santa Claus Lane!
He'll come around when the chimes ring out, then it's Christmas morn again.
Peace on earth will come to all if we just follow the light.
Let's give thanks to the Lord above, 'cause Santa Claus comes tonight!

A HOLLY JOLLY CHRISTMAS

Words and Music by
JOHNNY MARKS
Arranged by DAN COATES

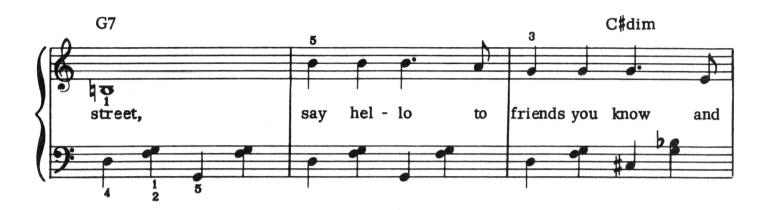

street, say hel - lo to friends you know and

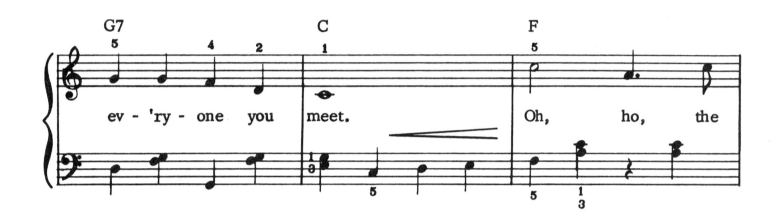

ev - 'ry - one you meet. Oh, ho, the

mis - tle - toe hung where you can see.

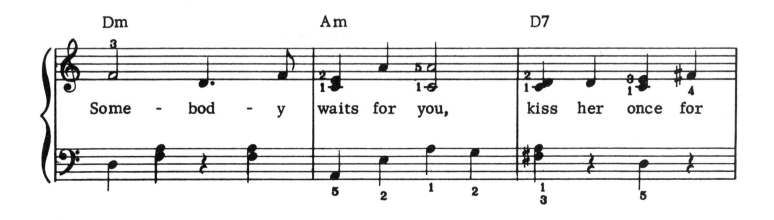

Some - bod - y waits for you, kiss her once for

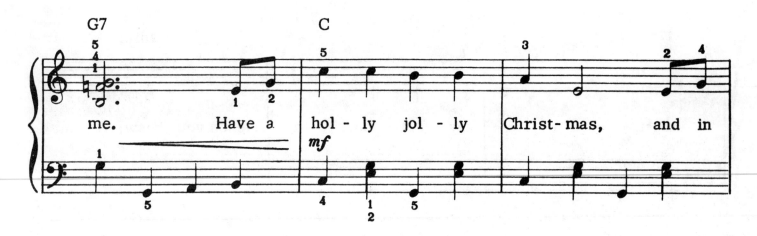

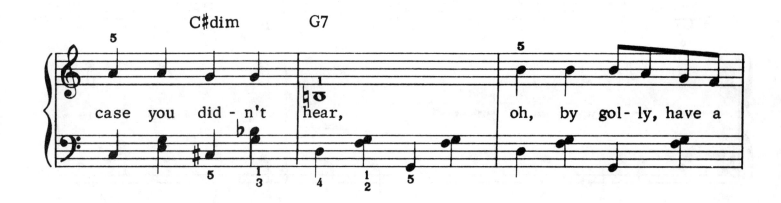

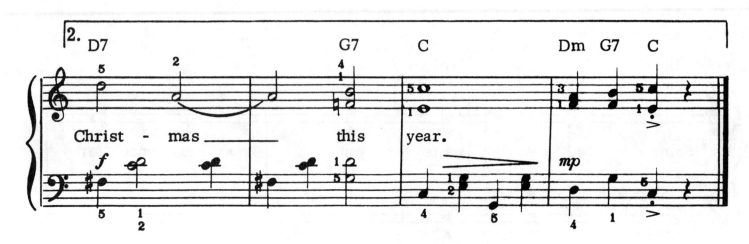

(There's No Place Like)
HOME FOR THE HOLIDAYS

Words by
AL STILLMAN

Music by
ROBERT ALLEN
Arranged by DAN COATES

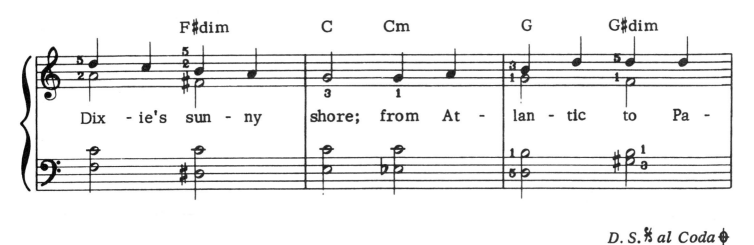

D. S. ℅ al Coda ⊕

Coda

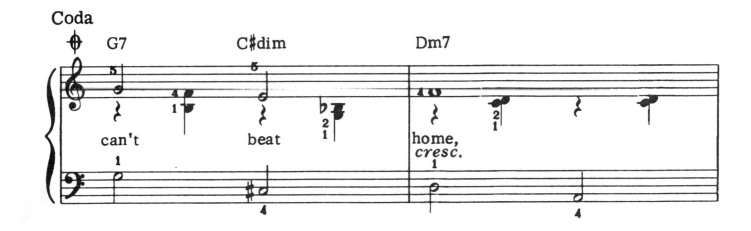

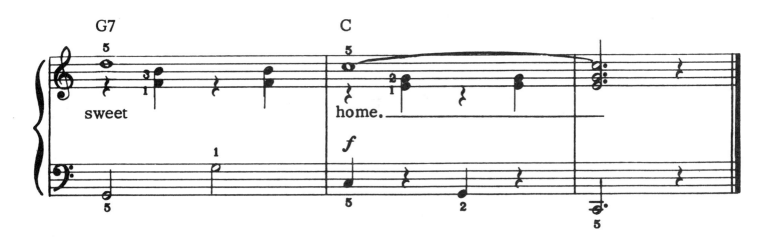

I BELIEVE IN SANTA CLAUS

Words by
HAL DAVID

Music by
MORTY NEVINS
Arranged by DAN COATES

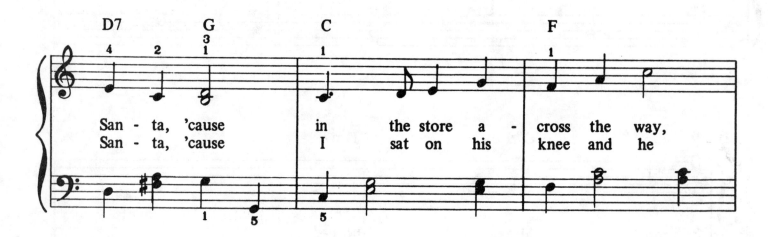

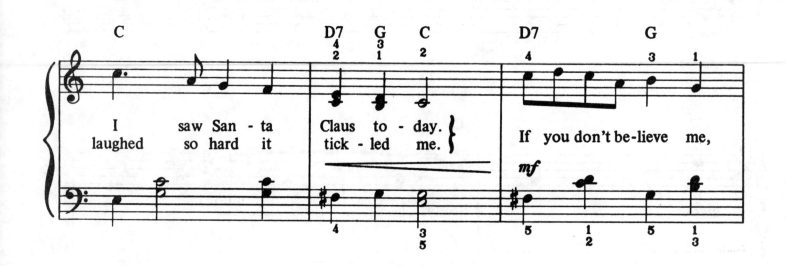

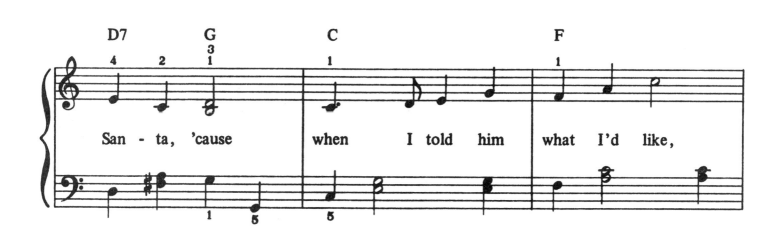

if you don't be-lieve me, you can go and see him for your-self.

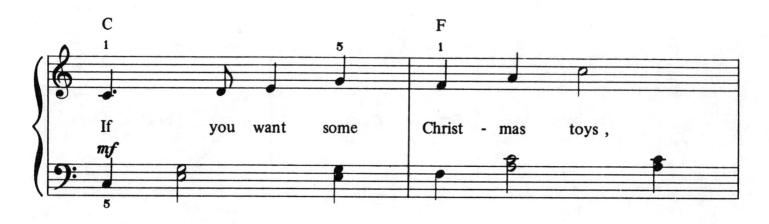

If you want some Christ - mas toys,

don't you laugh at San - ta, 'cause toys are just for

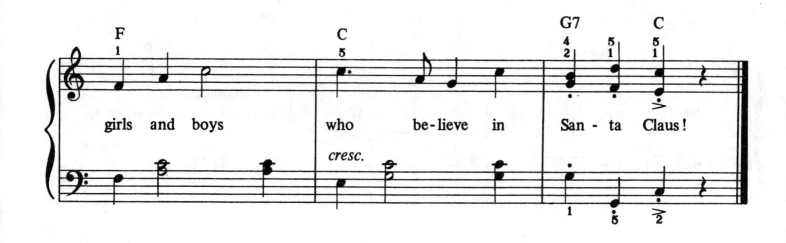

girls and boys who be-lieve in San - ta Claus!

IT'S THE MOST WONDERFUL
TIME OF THE YEAR

By
EDDIE POLA and GEORGE WYLE
Arranged by DAN COATES

I HEARD THE BELLS ON CHRISTMAS DAY

Words by
HENRY WADSWORTH LONGFELLOW
(Adapted by JOHNNY MARKS)

Music by
JOHNNY MARKS
Arranged by DAN COATES

I'LL BE HOME FOR CHRISTMAS

Words by
KIM GANNON

Music by
WALTER KENT
Arranged by DAN COATES

I'LL WALK WITH GOD

Words by
PAUL FRANCIS WEBSTER

Music by
NICHOLAS BRODSZKY
Arranged by DAN COATES

JINGLE BELLS

Traditional
Arranged by DAN COATES

LET IT SNOW! LET IT SNOW! LET IT SNOW!

Lyric by
SAMMY CAHN

Music by
JULE STYNE
Arranged by DAN COATES

INFANT SO GENTLE

Gascon Carol
Arranged by DAN COATES

1. In - fant so gen - tle, so pure and so sweet,___ Love from Thy ti - ny eyes sin - ners doth___ greet.
2. In - fant so ho - ly, so meek and so mild,___ We come to wel - come Thee, our___ dear Christ___ child.

Ten - d'rest words fail all Thy beau - ty to show,___
We can - not tell Thee how much we do need,___

We must a - dore Thee, if Thee___ we would___ know.
Thy pre - cious pres - ence; all sin - ners take___ heed.

LITTLE CHILDREN, CAN YOU TELL?

Anonymous
Arranged by DAN COATES

THE LITTLE DRUMMER BOY

Words and Music by
KATHERINE DAVIS, HENRY ONORATI
and HARRY SIMEONE
Arranged by DAN COATES

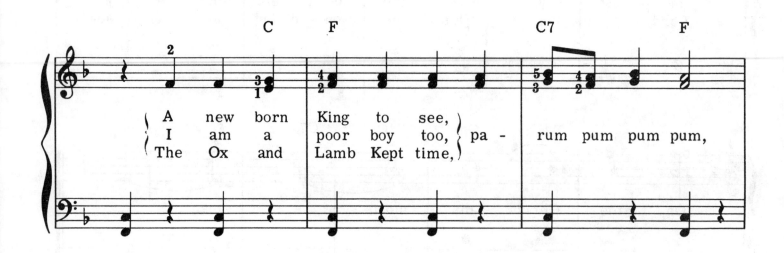

MERRY CHRISTMAS, DARLING

Lyrics by
FRANK POOLER

Music by
RICHARD CARPENTER
Arranged by DAN COATES

A MERRY, MERRY CHRISTMAS TO YOU
(Joyeux Noel, Buon Natale, Feliz Navidad)

By
JOHNNY MARKS
Arranged by DAN COATES

Very spirited

THE MOST WONDERFUL DAY OF THE YEAR

Words and Music by
JOHNNY MARKS
Arranged by DAN COATES

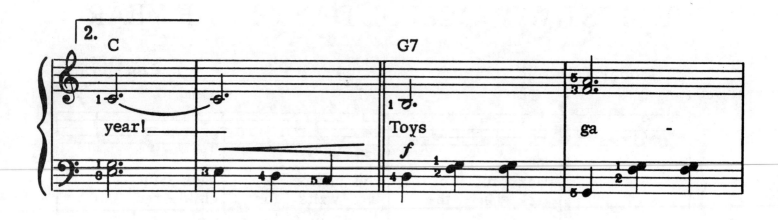

2. C · G7

year! _____ Toys ga -

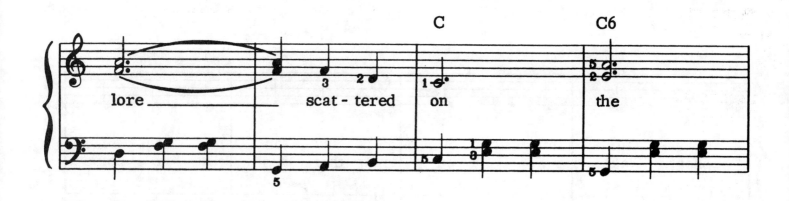

C   C6

lore _____ scat - tered on the

D7

floor. _____ There's no room for

G9   C#dim7

more, _____ and it's all be - cause of

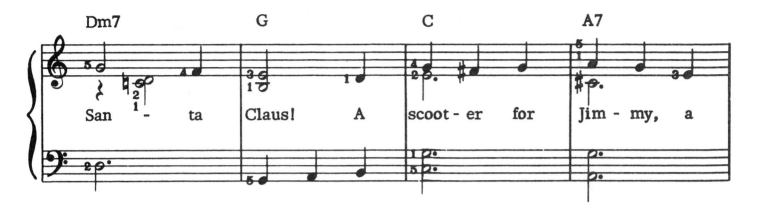

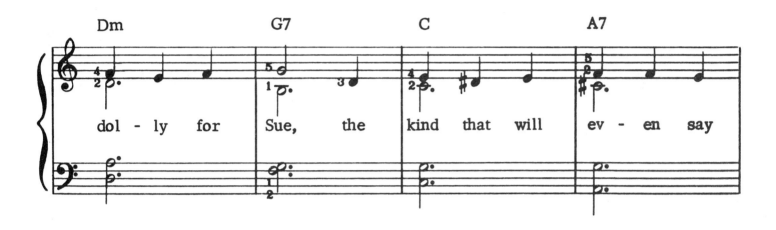

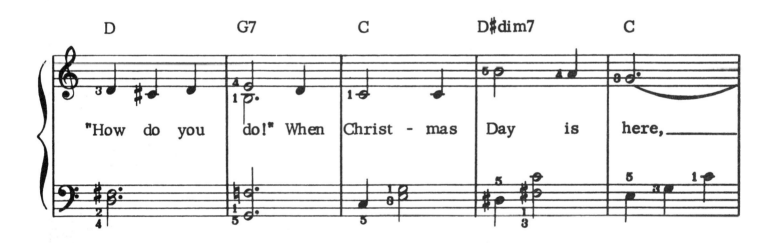

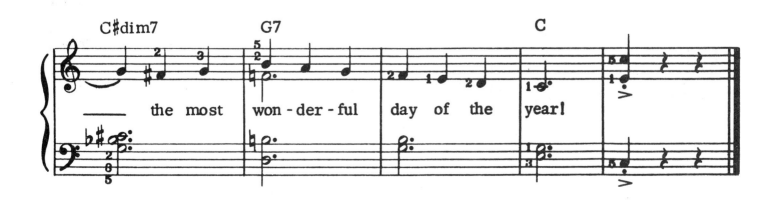

O COME, O COME EMMANUEL

Traditional
Arranged by DAN COATES

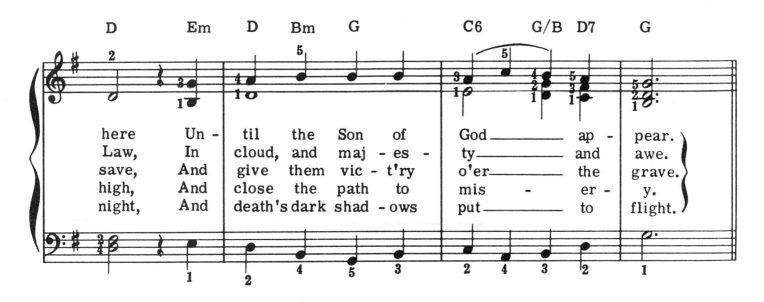

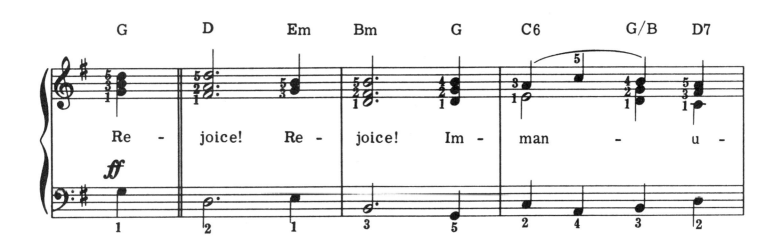

THE NIGHT BEFORE CHRISTMAS SONG

Lyric adapted by
JOHNNY MARKS
From Clement Moore's Poem

Music by
JOHNNY MARKS
Arranged by DAN COATES

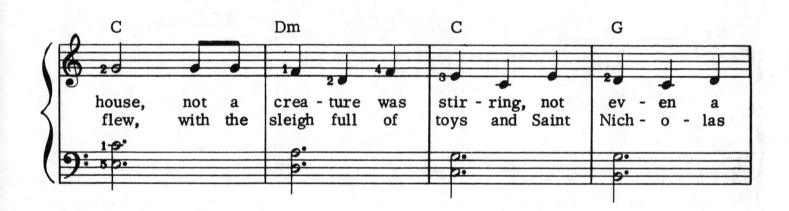

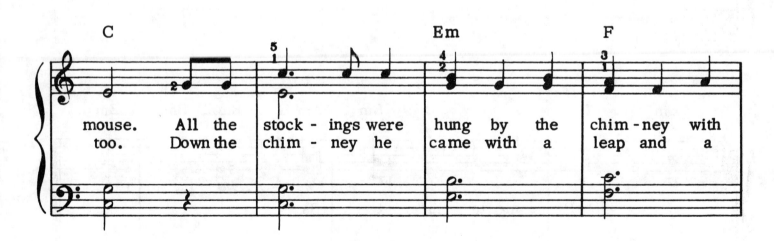

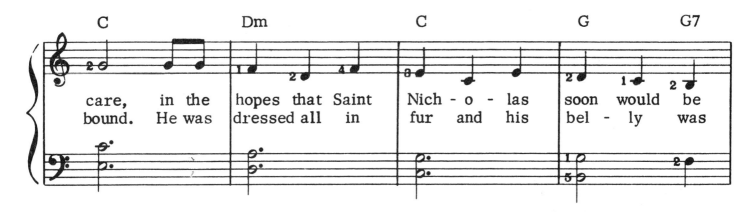

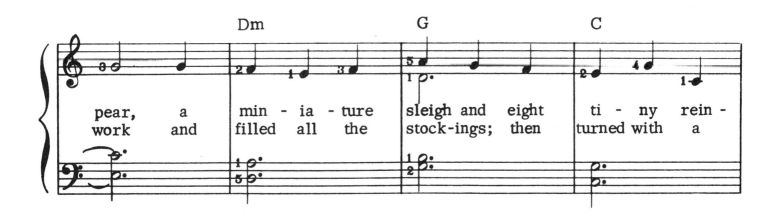

O LITTLE TOWN OF BETHLEHEM

Words by
PHILLIPS BROOKS

Music by
LEWIS H. REDNER
Arranged by DAN COATES

ROCKIN' AROUND
THE CHRISTMAS TREE

Words and Music by
JOHNNY MARKS
Arranged by DAN COATES

Moderately, with a rock

Rock-in' a - round the Christ-mas tree__ at the Christ-mas par - ty hop. Mis-tle-toe hung where you can see__ ev - 'ry cou - ple tries to stop. Rock-in' a - round the Christ-mas tree,__ let the Christ-mas spir - it

ring. Lat-er we'll have some pump-kin pie __ and we'll

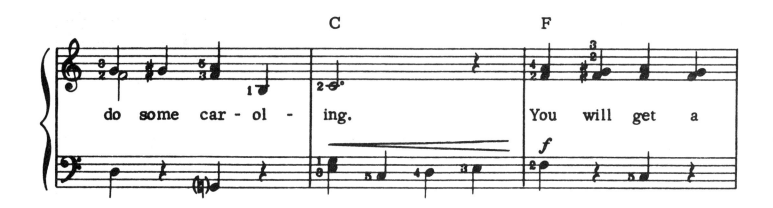

C   F

do some car - ol - ing.   You will get a

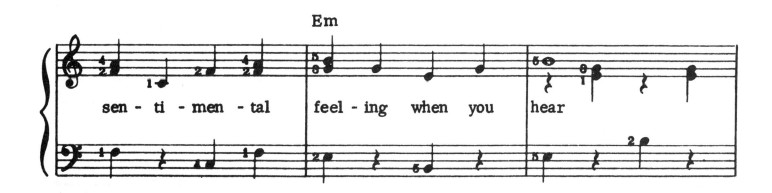

Em

sen - ti - men - tal   feel - ing when you   hear

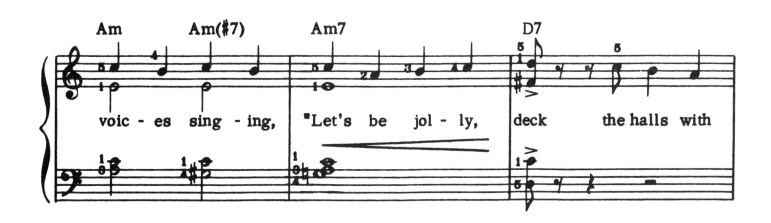

Am   Am(#7)   Am7   D7

voic - es sing - ing,   "Let's be jol - ly,   deck   the halls with

RUDOLPH,
THE RED-NOSED REINDEER

Words and Music by
JOHNNY MARKS
Arranged by DAN COATES

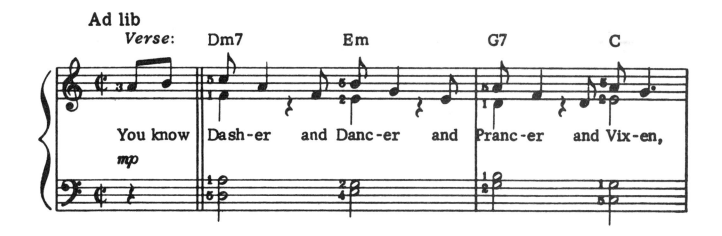

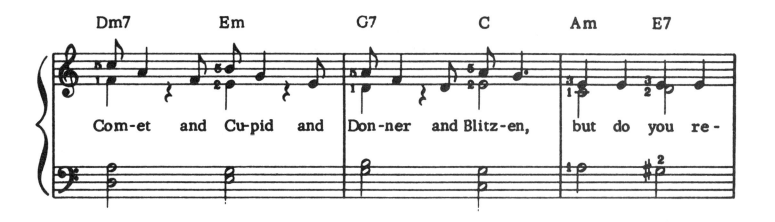

Lightly

Chorus:

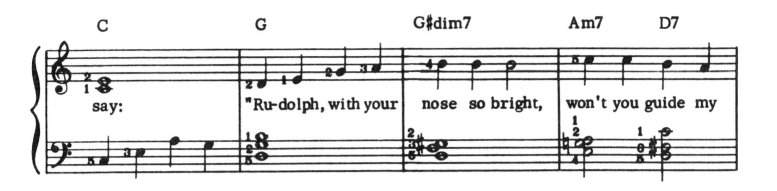

C   G   G#dim7   Am7   D7

say: "Ru-dolph, with your nose so bright, won't you guide my

G7   C

sleigh to -night?_ Then how the rein-deer loved him

Cdim   G7

as they shout-ed out with glee: "Ru-dolph, the red-nosed

C

rein - deer, you'll go down in his - to - ry."

SANTA CLAUS IS COMIN' TO TOWN

Words by
HAVEN GILLESPIE

Music by
J. FRED COOTS
Arranged by DAN COATES

SANTA CLAUS IS BACK IN TOWN

Words and Music by
JERRY LEIBER and MIKE STOLLER

(Christ-mas,_____ Christ-mas,_____ Christ-mas._____)

Chorus:

Well, it's Christ-mas time,_ pret-ty ba - by,

and the snow is fall-ing on the ground._____

Well, it's Christ-mas time,__ pret-ty ba - by,

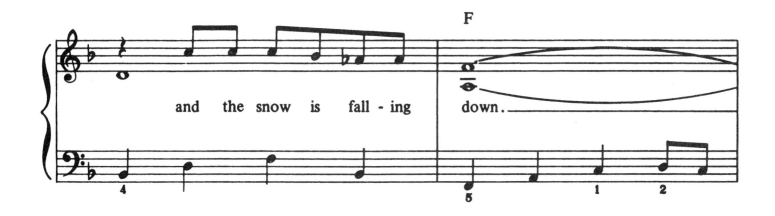

and the snow is fall - ing down.__

Well, you be a real good__ lit-tle girl.

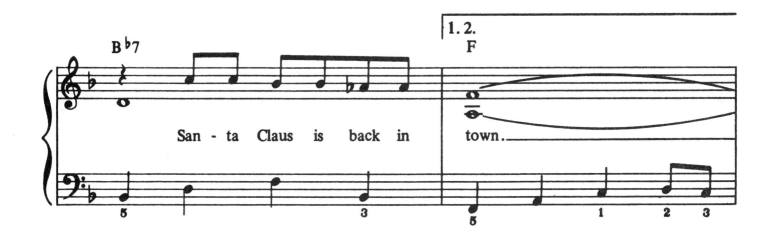

San - ta Claus is back in town.__

SILENT NIGHT

Words by
JOSEPH MOHR

Music by
FRANZ GRUBER
Arranged by DAN COATES

THERE IS NO CHRISTMAS
LIKE A HOME CHRISTMAS

Words by
CARL SIGMAN

Music by
MICKEY J. ADDY
Arranged by DAN COATES

SING WE NOËL

French Carol
Arranged by DAN COATES

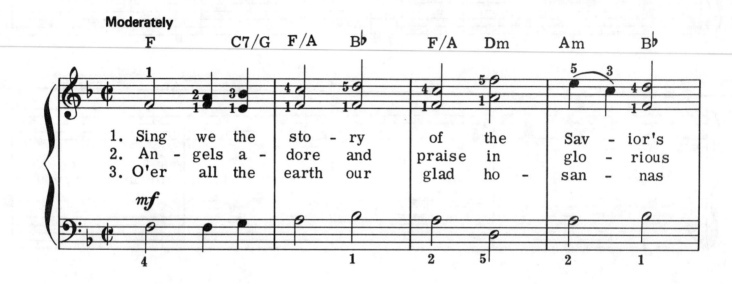

1. Sing we the sto - ry of the Sav - ior's
2. An - gels a - dore and praise in glo - rious
3. O'er all the earth our glad ho - san - nas

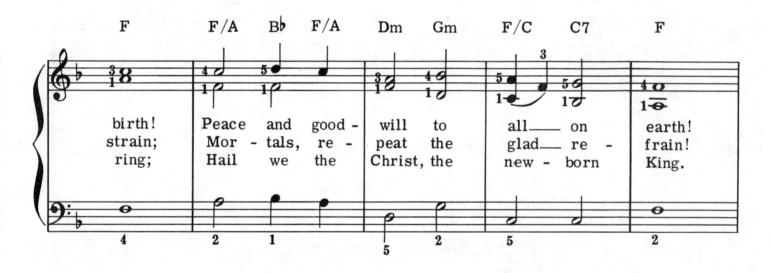

birth! Peace and good - will to all___ on earth!
strain; Mor - tals, re - peat the glad___ re - frain!
ring; Hail we the Christ, the new - born King.

Laud and a - dore the Vir - gin pure___ and mild,
Bright in the East a fair and shin - ing star,
Shout the glad ti - dings of the Sav - ior's birth,

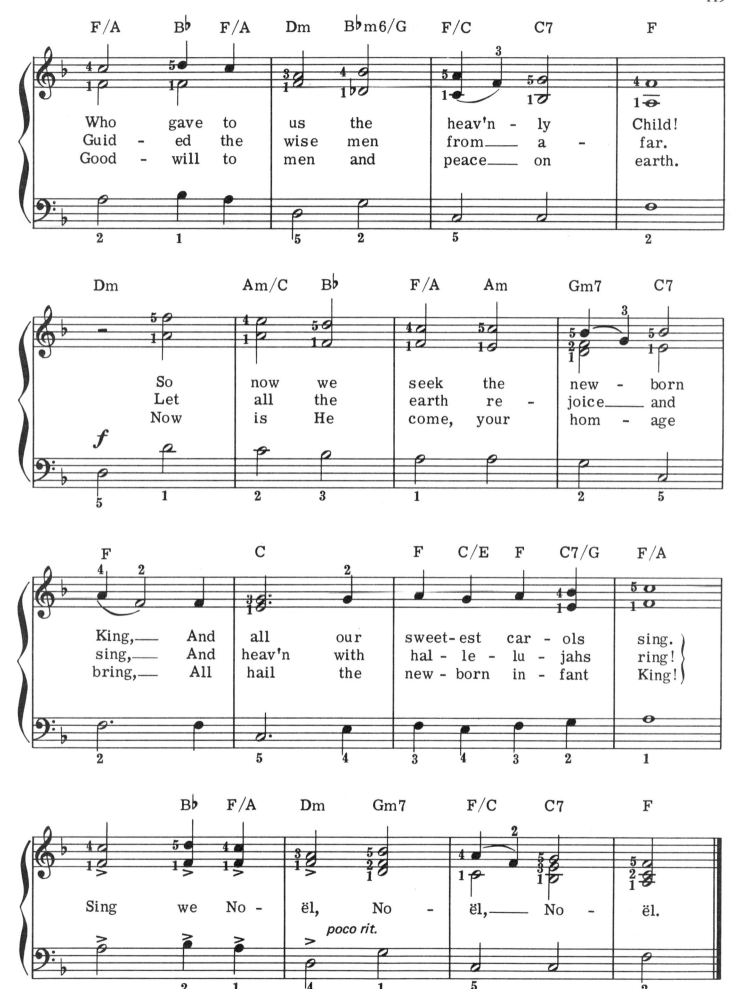

SLEIGH RIDE

Words by
MITCHELL PARISH

Music by
LEROY ANDERSON
Arranged by DAN COATES

WE WISH YOU A MERRY CHRISTMAS

Traditional English Folk Song
Arranged by DAN COATES

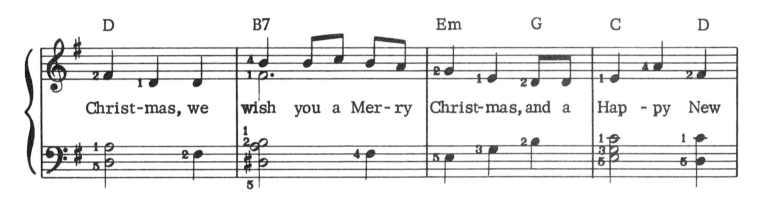

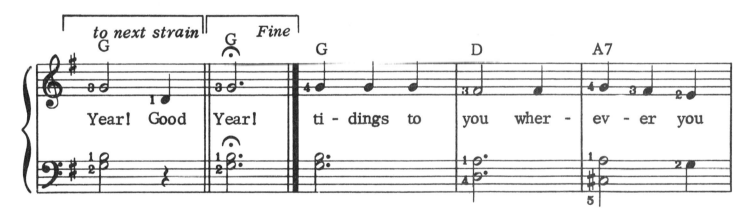

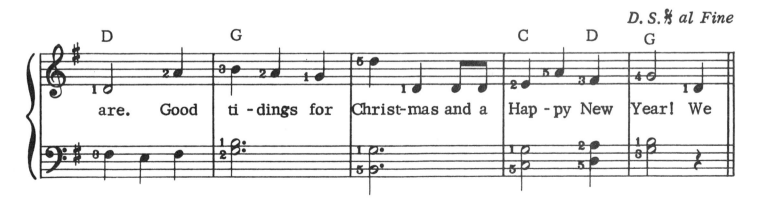

WHILE SHEPHERDS WATCHED THEIR FLOCKS

Adapted from Handel
Arranged by DAN COATES

Additional Lyrics

3. "To you, in David's town, this day is born of David's line,
   The Savior who is Christ the Lord; and this shall be the sign,
   And this shall be the sign.

4. "The heavenly Babe you there shall find to human view displayed,
   All meanly wrapped in swathing bands, and in a manger laid,
   And in a manger laid."

WINTER WONDERLAND

Words by
DICK SMITH

Music by
FELIX BERNARD
Arranged by DAN COATES

sings a love song,—}
sing-ing a song,—} as we go a-long,—— walk-in' in a win-ter won-der-

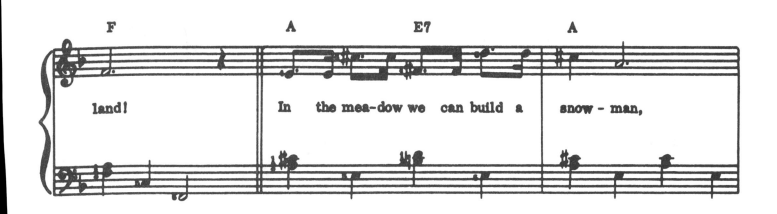

land! In the mea-dow we can build a snow-man,

{Then pre-tend that he is Par-son Brown;
{And pre-tend that he's a cir-cus clown;

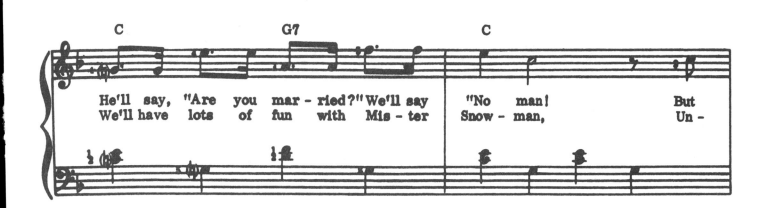

He'll say, "Are you mar-ried?" We'll say "No man! But
We'll have lots of fun with Mis-ter Snow-man, Un-

you can do the job when you're in town!" Lat - er
til the oth - er kid - dies knock 'im down! When it

on, we'll con - spire,___ As we dream by the
snows, ain't it thrill - in', Though your nose gets a

fire,___ To face un - a - fraid, the plans that we made,
chill - in'? We'll frol - ic and play the es - ki - mo way,

walk - in' in a win - ter won - der - land! Sleigh bells land!